25 Days of Bible Verses for Praise & Thankfulness

A CHRISTIAN DEVOTIONAL & COLORING JOURNAL

written & designed by Shalana Frisby

More information at: www.123journalit.com

First Printing: October 2018
1 2 3 Journal It Publishing

ISBN-13: 978-1-947209-90-9
25 Days of Bible Verses Series: Praise & Thankfulness Edition

This journal belongs to

How to use this journal:

Find a quiet place and start with prayer asking for guidance.

Write the included daily verses using your preferred bible version.

Dig deeper by filling in the sections on the study notes page.

Journal reflections about life and your additional notes.

Get creative by coloring, doodling, and drawing.

...have fun hiding God's Word in your heart...

Write, Reflect, & Repeat Daily

The 25 Bible Verses Featured:

1 Chronicles 16:34-36

Colossians 3:15-17

Jeremiah 33:10-11

2 Corinthians 2:14-16

Isaiah 12:1-3

Isaiah 12-4-6

Hebrews 12:28-29

Psalm 100:1-5

Philippians 4:4-7

Daniel 2:19-23

1 Timothy 4:3-5

Jonah 2:7-9

1 Thessalonians 5:16-18

Psalm 95:1-2

2 Corinthians 9:12-15

Psalm 75: 1 & 9

Revelation 7:11-12

Colossians 2:6-7

1 Chronicles 16:8-10

Ephesians 5:3-4

Revelation 11:16-17

Jeremiah 30:18-19

Colossians 4:2-6

John 11:40-42

John 3:16-18

PRAY & WRITE TODAY'S VERSE:
1 Chronicles 16:34-36

STUDY NOTES: what does this scripture mean?

TODAY'S date: _____________

PRAYER REQUESTS
& praise for answered prayers:

DIG DEEPER: how does it apply to my life?

GIVE THANKS
what I'm grateful for today:

REFLECTIONS & NOTES:

PRAY & WRITE TODAY'S VERSE:

Colossians 3:15-17

STUDY NOTES: what does this scripture mean?

____

TODAY'S date: _______________

PRAYER REQUESTS
& praise for answered prayers:

DIG DEEPER: how does it apply to my life?

____

GIVE THANKS
what I'm grateful for today:

REFLECTIONS & NOTES:

PRAY & WRITE TODAY'S VERSE:
Jeremiah 33:10-11

STUDY NOTES: *what does this scripture mean?*

TODAY'S *date:* _______________

PRAYER REQUESTS
& praise for answered prayers:

DIG DEEPER: *how does it apply to my life?*

GIVE THANKS
what I'm grateful for today:

REFLECTIONS & NOTES:

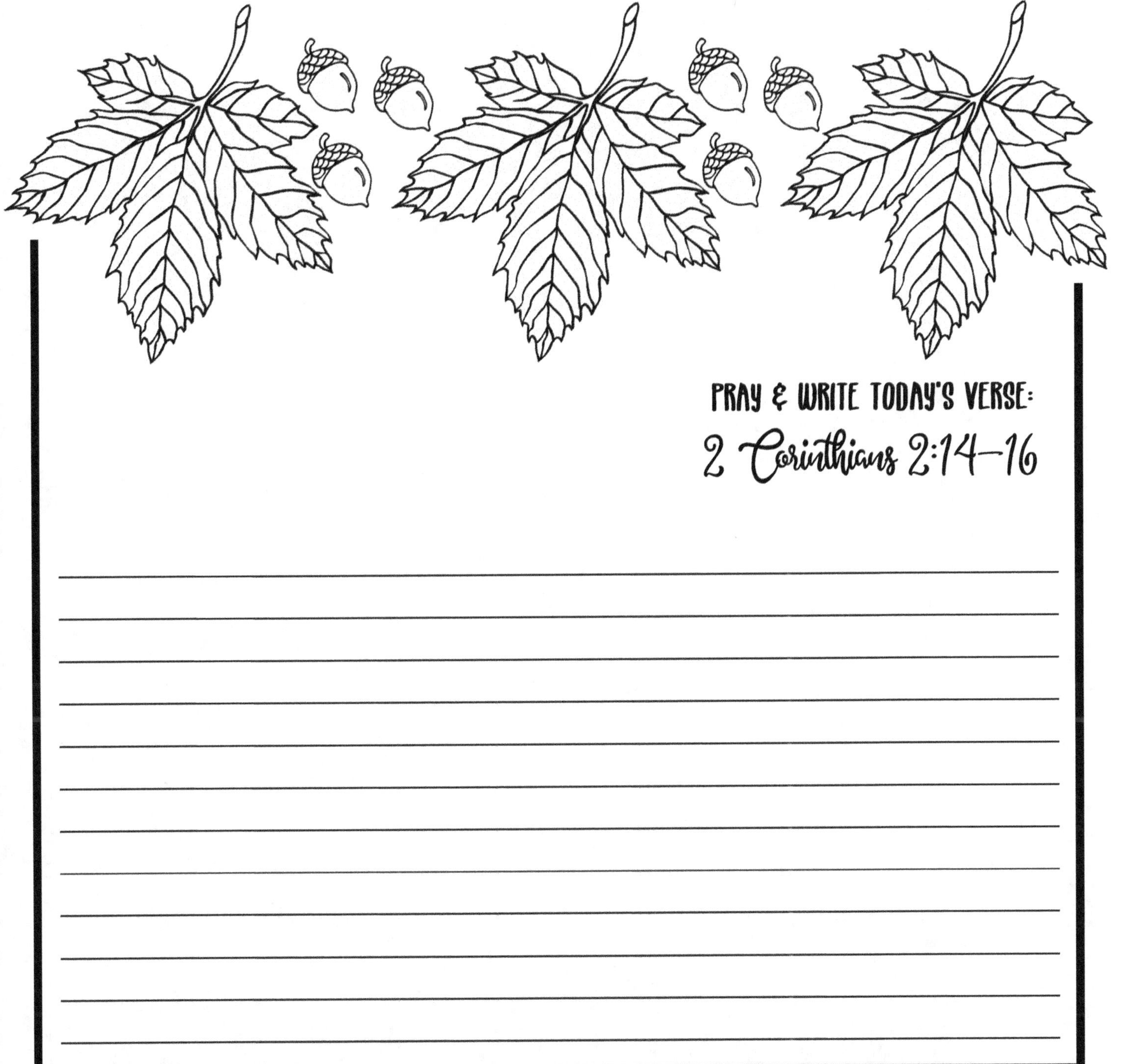

PRAY & WRITE TODAY'S VERSE:
2 Corinthians 2:14-16

STUDY NOTES: what does this scripture mean?

TODAY'S date: _______________

PRAYER REQUESTS
& praise for answered prayers:

DIG DEEPER: how does it apply to my life?

GIVE THANKS
what I'm grateful for today:

REFLECTIONS & NOTES:

PRAY & WRITE TODAY'S VERSE:
Isaiah 12:1-3

STUDY NOTES: what does this scripture mean?

TODAY'S date: _____________

DIG DEEPER: how does it apply to my life?

PRAY & WRITE TODAY'S VERSE:
Isaiah 12:4-6

STUDY NOTES: what does this scripture mean?

TODAY'S date: _______________

PRAYER REQUESTS
& praise for answered prayers:

DIG DEEPER: how does it apply to my life?

GIVE THANKS
what I'm grateful for today:

REFLECTIONS & NOTES:

PRAY & WRITE TODAY'S VERSE:
Hebrews 12:28-29

STUDY NOTES: *what does this scripture mean?*

TODAY'S *date:* _______________

PRAYER REQUESTS
& praise for answered prayers:

DIG DEEPER: *how does it apply to my life?*

GIVE THANKS
what I'm grateful for today:

REFLECTIONS & NOTES:

PRAY & WRITE TODAY'S VERSE:
Psalm 100:1-5

STUDY NOTES: what does this scripture mean?

TODAY'S date: _____________

PRAYER REQUESTS
& praise for answered prayers:

DIG DEEPER: how does it apply to my life?

GIVE THANKS
what I'm grateful for today:

PRAY & WRITE TODAY'S VERSE:
Philippians 4:4-7

STUDY NOTES: *what does this scripture mean?*

____

DIG DEEPER: *how does it apply to my life?*

____

PRAYER REQUESTS
& praise for answered prayers:

GIVE THANKS
what I'm grateful for today:

REFLECTIONS & NOTES:

PRAY & WRITE TODAY'S VERSE:
Daniel 2:19-23

STUDY NOTES: what does this scripture mean?

TODAY'S date: __________

PRAYER REQUESTS
& praise for answered prayers:

DIG DEEPER: how does it apply to my life?

GIVE THANKS
what I'm grateful for today:

REFLECTIONS & NOTES:

PRAY & WRITE TODAY'S VERSE:
1 Timothy 4:3-5

STUDY NOTES: what does this scripture mean?

____
____
____
____
____
____
____
____
____

DIG DEEPER: how does it apply to my life?

____
____
____
____
____
____
____

TODAY'S date: _____________

PRAYER REQUESTS
& praise for answered prayers:

GIVE THANKS
what I'm grateful for today:

REFLECTIONS & NOTES:

PRAY & WRITE TODAY'S VERSE:
Jonah 2:7-9

STUDY NOTES: what does this scripture mean?

TODAY'S date: _______________

PRAYER REQUESTS
& praise for answered prayers:

DIG DEEPER: how does it apply to my life?

GIVE THANKS
what I'm grateful for today:

PRAY & WRITE TODAY'S VERSE:
1 Thessalonians 5:16-18

STUDY NOTES: what does this scripture mean?

TODAY'S date: _____________

DIG DEEPER: how does it apply to my life?

REFLECTIONS & NOTES:

PRAY & WRITE TODAY'S VERSE:
Psalm 95:1-2

STUDY NOTES: what does this scripture mean?

TODAY'S date: _______________

PRAYER REQUESTS
& praise for answered prayers:

DIG DEEPER: how does it apply to my life?

GIVE THANKS
what I'm grateful for today:

REFLECTIONS & NOTES:

PRAY & WRITE TODAY'S VERSE:
2 Corinthians 9:12-15

STUDY NOTES: *what does this scripture mean?*

TODAY'S *date:* ___________

PRAYER REQUESTS
& praise for answered prayers:

DIG DEEPER: *how does it apply to my life?*

GIVE THANKS
what I'm grateful for today:

REFLECTIONS & NOTES:

PRAY & WRITE TODAY'S VERSE:

Psalm 75:1 & 9

STUDY NOTES: what does this scripture mean?

TODAY'S date: _______________

PRAYER REQUESTS
& praise for answered prayers:

DIG DEEPER: how does it apply to my life?

GIVE THANKS
what I'm grateful for today:

PRAY & WRITE TODAY'S VERSE:
Revelation 7:11-12

STUDY NOTES: what does this scripture mean?

TODAY'S date: _______________

PRAYER REQUESTS
& praise for answered prayers:

DIG DEEPER: how does it apply to my life?

GIVE THANKS
what I'm grateful for today:

REFLECTIONS & NOTES:

PRAY & WRITE TODAY'S VERSE:
Colossians 2:6-7

STUDY NOTES: what does this scripture mean?

TODAY'S date: _______________

PRAYER REQUESTS
& praise for answered prayers:

DIG DEEPER: how does it apply to my life?

GIVE THANKS
what I'm grateful for today:

PRAY & WRITE TODAY'S VERSE:
1 Chronicles 16:8-10

STUDY NOTES: what does this scripture mean?

____

PRAYER REQUESTS
& praise for answered prayers:

....
....
....
....
....
....
....

DIG DEEPER: how does it apply to my life?

____

GIVE THANKS
what I'm grateful for today:

....
....
....
....
....
....
....

PRAY & WRITE TODAY'S VERSE:
Ephesians 5:3-4

STUDY NOTES: what does this scripture mean?

TODAY'S date: _____________

PRAYER REQUESTS
& praise for answered prayers:

DIG DEEPER: how does it apply to my life?

GIVE THANKS
what I'm grateful for today:

REFLECTIONS & NOTES:

Revelation 11:16–17

STUDY NOTES: what does this scripture mean?

TODAY'S date: _______________

PRAYER REQUESTS
& praise for answered prayers:

DIG DEEPER: how does it apply to my life?

GIVE THANKS
what I'm grateful for today:

PRAY & WRITE TODAY'S VERSE:
Jeremiah 30:18-19

STUDY NOTES: what does this scripture mean?

TODAY'S date: _____________

PRAYER REQUESTS
& praise for answered prayers:

DIG DEEPER: how does it apply to my life?

GIVE THANKS
what I'm grateful for today:

REFLECTIONS & NOTES:

PRAY & WRITE TODAY'S VERSE:
Colossians 4:2-6

STUDY NOTES: *what does this scripture mean?*

TODAY'S *date:* _______________

DIG DEEPER: *how does it apply to my life?*

REFLECTIONS & NOTES:

PRAY & WRITE TODAY'S VERSE:
John 11:40-42

STUDY NOTES: what does this scripture mean?

TODAY'S date: _____________

PRAYER REQUESTS
& praise for answered prayers:

DIG DEEPER: how does it apply to my life?

GIVE THANKS
what I'm grateful for today:

REFLECTIONS & NOTES:

PRAY & WRITE TODAY'S VERSE:
John 3:16-18

STUDY NOTES: what does this scripture mean?

PRAYER REQUESTS
& praise for answered prayers:

DIG DEEPER: how does it apply to my life?

GIVE THANKS
what I'm grateful for today:

REFLECTIONS & NOTES: